Donald Trump

Donald Trump's best lessons for life, business, and success!

Table of Contents

Introduction

Thank you for taking the time to pick up this book: Donald Trump.

This book talks about the story of Donald Trump, and shares some of his greatest lessons for life.

At the completion of this book you will have a good understanding of Donald's incredible journey, and will be able to use his experiences to enhance your own life!

You will learn all about his biggest business successes, along with failures. Trump's long and diverse career is full of a multitude of lessons that will be able to improve your abilities as an entrepreneur and also as a marketer.

Trump's political campaign is also discussed, and you will learn about his different ideologies and political strategies.

Once again, thanks for choosing this book, I hope you find it to be interesting!

Chapter 1:
The Man, The Persona

Few people in America's entrepreneurial history have been as inspiring, brazen, flamboyant and controversial as Donald Trump. The businessman, who dons the multiple hats of a television personality, presidential candidate and author, heads The Trump Organization that boasts of innumerable real estate projects and other lucrative business interests. The Republican Party's presumptive nominee for the 2016 presidential election, Trump's a graduate of the Wharton School of the University of Pennsylvania.

The Unusual Persona

Trump's journey of a thousand miles began when he started working at his father – Fred Trump's construction and real estate firm, while still in college. His astute business sense and razor sharp strategic thinking abilities coupled with ambition and a fearless approach helped him assume absolute control of the enterprise in 1973, renaming it to The Trump Organization.

Forging a strong identity for his brand in a short time, the real estate magnate made his company a force to reckon with by dipping his business savvy hands into a number of ventures ranging from vacation resorts to state of the art golf courses to popular beauty pageants. Today, though his brands are licensed to several other businesses in which he holds minimal or zero stake, the brand value is unmistakably high and unique. That is the power anything associated with his name commands.

The Media's Favorite Prime Time Boy

The media's favorite prime time television boy, Trump has rarely been shy of courting incessant news bytes and controversies for his larger than life personal and professional life. His three marriages to Ivana Zelnickova, Marla Maples and Melinia Knauss garnered as much attention as his far-sighted business acquisitions. Trump has featured consistently on the Forbes list of the world's 400 richest billionaires, and hosted a popular reality television show, *The Apprentice* on NBC for over a decade.

Fascinating Early Life Details

Born on June, 14, 1946,at Jamaica Estates, a New York City neighborhood, Donald Trump was born to Mary Trump and Fred Trump, and is the fourth in a family of five children. Though there have been discrepancies about his ancestry, with some incorrectly attributing a Swedish lineage, Trump himself cleared the air by accepting his German roots. Though his father Fred Trump spoke to an interviewer about Donald being a "pretty rough fellow" as a child, Donald Trump went on to participate in marching drills, sporting a uniform and gaining a captain's rank while in his senior year.

How did he charter such an inspiring and incredible journey that raked in millions for his organization? What are the traits that set this infallible man aside? What are the primary lessons to be learnt and emulated from life? Read on to find more interesting details about Donald Trump's life.

Chapter 2:
Conquering the Real Estate World

Even before he graduated, Trump was working hands-on at his father's real estate firm, Elizabeth Trump and Son. The company primarily offered mid-range rental housing services in New York City. One of Trump's earliest ventures was renewing a foreclosed apartment complex in Cincinnati that his father bought for close to $5.7 million in 1962. The 1200 unit residential complex with a $500,000 investment witnessed its occupancy level rise from 34% to a staggering 100% after Donald Trump got involved hands-on with the venture. The Swifton Village Complex was later sold for a whopping $6.75 million.

The Aesthetics

Unlike other real estate magnates, Trump recognized the power of aesthetics and lent his projects cutting-edge architectural designs that won them instant recognition and widespread publicity. By 1973, Trump was already president of the booming Trump Organization, and supervised 14,000 apartment units all across middle-class New York boroughs such as Queens, Staten Island and Brooklyn.

The Grand Hyatt Hotel

His first big moment of glory arrived in the form of a lucrative Manhattan deal of the Grand Hyatt Hotel building in 1978. Trump whisked his way into the limelight with this power deal that set to transform the fledging fortune of the Penn Central Transportation Company owned Commodore Hotel. Donald also successfully negotiated a four-decade long tax rebate for a stake in the enterprise's profits. This smart move not just lowered the venture's risk, but also encouraged investors to hop aboard with certainty.

The Iconic Trump Tower

Donald Trump once again showcased his shrewd negotiation skills and persistence when he successfully pulled off an iconic project that comprised complex negotiations with for various spaces, including the Bonwit Teller structure, the neighboring building airspace and the land. The very fact that Trump was able to bag such a complicated and prestigious location spoke a lot about his vision, astute negotiations and unwavering single-mindedness.

Trump Tower is a magnificent architectural masterpiece that's considered one of New York City's most enviable addresses. It is a 58-story skyscraper, located on the posh Fifth Avenue in Manhattan. Designed by renowned architect Der Scutt, it features the headquarters of The Trump Organization and is the primary residence of Donald Trump.

The structure houses, amongst other chic facilities such as boutiques, offices, coffee shops and residences. There's a multi-level atrium and a 60-foot waterfall (replete with a walkway under a skylight) to complete the picture of high living standards, that's been the hallmark of a majority of Trump's ventures. The imposing structure is nothing short of a tourist attraction today, and acted as a glittery backdrop for *The Apprentice,* which was shot within the tower's fully equipped television studio.

Trump Tower went on to occupy the architectural site of the Bonwit Teller flagship store that was razed down in 1980. A huge uproar ensued when priceless Art Deco sculptures from the façade, which were supposed to be showcased at the Metropolitan Museum of Art were destroyed during demolition. Another controversy erupted when it was discovered that Polish immigrant workers were hired at $4-5 an hour for extended 12-hour shifts.

Trump gave a testimony in 1990 that he didn't visit the site and was not aware of the illegal migrants. In 1991, a judge ruled that the builders engaged in a deliberate conspiracy to deprive the workers of their welfare funds, wages and pension. Some sections of the ruling were overturned on appeal. The extended labor lawsuit finally reached a settlement in 1999.

Trump's Holiday Properties

There was no stopping the real estate magnate, with acquisitions ranging from the Trump Plaza Hotel/Casino in Atlantic City (1984) to the Mar-a-Lago estate at Palm Beach, Florida (1985) to Plaza Hotel in New York City's Central Park neighborhood. The Florida property was perceptively also converted into an elite private club with a $150,000 membership tag.

This reveals the man's innate sense of recognizing opportunities and creating ventures that catered to people's needs, which they didn't even believe existed. Trump sensed business opportunities with the tenacity of a hound and went after them head on until their fullest potential was realized.

Chapter 3:
The Entertainment Media Whiz

Until he recently sold off his stake in the Miss Universe, Miss Teen USA and Miss USA, Donald Trump held part or absolute ownership of these popular beauty pageants. From 1996 to 2015, these events, with their share of controversies and uproars, were managed by Trump's organization. He received all-round criticism for allowing Miss USA winner Tara Conner to keep her crown, despite being tested positive for cocaine. Both NBC and Univision ended their association with the Miss Universe Organization after Trump's controversial presidential campaign kick-starter speech.

Movie Appearances

Trump's love affair with the spotlight strengthened with his special movie and innumerable television appearances. He has been nominated for an Emmy Award twice already. Other than being a Screen Actors Guild member and a constant subject for caricatures, the media star also hosted a daily radio show called *Trumped*.

One of the sharpest lessons to be picked up from the entrepreneurial brain of Donald Trump is his penchant for diversification. He never risked putting all his eggs into a single basket, and diversified his wealth into multiple income streams that include pensions, royalties and other long-term monetary streams. Trump's wealth model comprises different income streams that were incisively identified and pursued for maximum gain at the right time.

The Apprentice

2003 saw Donald Trump turning into an executive producer and anchor of the popular NBC reality show *'The Apprentice'* that consisted of a group of contestants vying for a prominent managerial job at one of Donald Trump's enterprises. The concept was a winner right from the onset. This combined with Trump's characteristic brazenness, where he freely fired and eliminated prospective employees from the game, won him a steady television viewership.

He even filed a trademark for his signature phrase on the show, "You're Fired". Trump never failed to recognize the power of his brand and always cashed in on it in time to gain as much as he could. He identified, recognized and never undermined the value his name could bring to the table, and always sought to make the most of it.

A year into its launch the show earned Trump a cool $50,000 per episode. Post the charismatic and savvy businessman's soaring prime time popularity, his paycheck grew to a staggering $1 million per episode. Trump's campaign manager went on record with a press release stating he made about $213,606, 575 for all 14 seasons of the show, though the claim wasn't attested by the network themselves. Again, an opportunity seized brilliantly by Donald Trump to create wealth resourcefully.

World Wrestling Entertainment

It's a known fact Trump is a huge World Wrestling Entertainment buff and close pal of the WWE owner Vince McMahon. Other than being an enthusiastic participant of many shows, Trump has also hosted a couple of WrestleMania events in the Trump Plaza. Trump made a rather unforgettable appearance in the Wrestle Mania23 match befittingly termed as "The Battle of the Billionaires". The challenge was that either Donald Trump or his buddy McMahon would shave their head if the competitor lost. Lashley ended up winning the bout, and McMahon got a haircut.

Controversial Documentary

A 2011 documentary film called *You've Been Trumped* generated considerable interest, owing to the fact that it tracked the progress of a Scottish golf resort. The film's telecast was sought to be halted by Trump's legal team on account of the film being defamatory and inaccurate. However, BBC Two still screened the film, and made a claim of Trump refusing to be a part of the documentary.

Chapter 4:
The Challenges

The real estate market began to plummet in the 1990s, thus decreasing the value of Trump's businesses. His individual net worth plunged from roughly $1.7 billion to $500 million. The Trump Organization sought heavy loans to keep their ventures afloat.

This challenging situation had many detractors contemplating whether it was wrap up time for The Trump Organization. While some experts attributed to the situation to rash business decisions, other simply saw it as an after effect of the 80s social excess phenomenon. Yet against all odds, Donald Trump rose like the proverbial phoenix from the ashes and reported a fortune of a staggering $2 billion in 1997.

Taj Mahal Casino

In 1988, Trump took over the Taj Mahal Casino in Atlantic City, New Jersey from Resorts International and Merv Griffin. The casino was built at a pricey sum of almost a billion dollars. The project went into Title 11 bankruptcy the subsequent year. The venture was resurrected from the tentacles of bankruptcy, releasing 50 percent ownership to bondholders for reduced interest rates and extended time to clear the debt.

He went to sell the non-performing Trump Shuttle airline and his prized yacht – Trump Princess to put things in order. The resort property was repurchased in the mid 90s and merged into Trump Hotels and Casino Resorts, which went on to file for bankruptcy in the early 2000s with a debt amounting to 1.8 billion.

The enterprise filed for bankruptcy again after five years, with $500 million in debt. Post the restructuring, Donald Trump was left with a 10% stake in Trump Taj Mahal and other casino properties under the Trump umbrella.

Trump has never had to file for personal bankruptcy, though his enterprises have been acknowledged as bankrupt about four times from 1991 to 2009. Even then, the sharp businessman that he is, Trump has always re-negotiated debt with banks and stock/bond holders, since Title 11 of bankruptcy permits negotiations.

Donald Trump has a keen understanding of bankruptcy laws and has used it incisively for his advantage. He has revealed the power of strategic thinking and problem solving in running a successful business. His demeanor points to the fact that even when it seems like the business is heading towards a dead end, one has to resort to resourceful thinking and creative solutions to bail out the enterprise rather than getting bogged down.

Legal Troubles

The Coalition for Responsible Development sued New York with infringement of zoning laws for permitting buildings to tower over other neighbourhood structures. Even though the city revamped its regulations to thwart other similar projects in the future, the state appeals court asserted Trump's right to complete an 856-foot condominium project on NYC's east side.

In 2010, Trump took former Miss Pennsylvania Sheena Monnin to court after she hurled allegations of the Miss USA 2012 pageant being rigged. The court directed her to pay

Trump a $5 million settlement. He also sued Palm Beach County for coercing the FAA to channelize air traffic above his home. The list also includes suing the Ossining town in New York for tax valuation of his golf course property there.

Chapter 5:
Hits and Misses

Like we saw in the previous chapter, everything hasn't always been hunky-dory where business is concerned even for an entrepreneur like Donald Trump. Each business empire has its share of hits and misses, and like Donald Trump has shown on multiple occasions, it is smart negotiations, strategic thinking and resourceful solutions that help your business get out of tricky situations.

The Money Spinners

Some of Trump's most inspiring hits have been his own books (18 titles to pick from) and his sharp brand licensing (his empire lends its name to prestigious real estate projects across the world to increase their value). The licences alone are worth about $562 million for the Trump empire. *The Donald J. Trump* is another brand from the stable that is a rage at Macy's. His acumen for the real estate trade remains unquestioned.

Other than growing the main holdings in New York City, Trump's company is also credited for renovating the Old Post Office near White House and the makeover of a historic building housed at 100 Pennsylvania Ave. NW to an upscale 270-room hotel.

Trump's Turkeys

Some of the disastrous products/services launched by Trump's empire include the Trump Airlines, which tried to put the signature Trump charisma on a field of Boeings in the 80's and

90's, only to fail miserably. Donald Trump's ambition of turning into a powerhouse mortgage lender didn't last beyond 18 months, thwarted by the housing bubble burst and the acute financial crisis. Trump Vodka was another product from the Trump label that tanked miserably.

Chapter 6:
A Politician Rises

Donald Trump's rise as a presidential nominee for the Republican Party is as phenomenal as his monumental growth as a businessman. Trump has had his political leanings and affiliations vary significantly over a period of time. He was also in the running as a Reform Party candidate. Some policy positions revised by him include taxation, government participation in health care and abortion.

Political Leanings

Though Donald Trump's political leanings before 1987 are not explicitly known, he was an ardent supporter of Republican candidate Ronald Reagan for U.S President in the 70s. Until he joined the Reform Party to run a presidential exploratory campaign for a nomination, Trump was a registered Republican. Due to the increasing influence of David Duke, Lenora Fulani and Pat Buchanan, he felt compelled to leave the party in 2001 and was a democrat for about nine years.

Once a Republican always a Republican seems to be the mantra with Donald Trump. He went back to being a Republican in 2009 after supporting Presidential candidate John McCain. Finally after a whirlwind of switching loyalties and political affiliations, Trump came back to the Republican Party after a five-month independent stint, and has vowed to stay there. His political leanings can best be articulated as contradictory, evolving and diverse.

2016 Presidential Campaign

If there's one thing that has brought the fading business giant from grip of oblivion, it's his controversial and rather limelight hogging 2016 presidential campaign. He first announced his nomination for presidential candidacy at the Trump Tower.

Love Him, Hate Him – There's No Ignoring Him

His contentious campaign is based mainly on issues focused around illegal immigration to the United States, outsourcing American jobs to other countries, combating Islamic terrorism, and the national debt. As a self-confessed conservative, his presidential campaign concentrates on American patriotism, with scant regard for political correctness.

The businessman is not known to mince his words, and has made a series of what were termed as "hate speeches" by his detractors during his campaign. Trump has had several allegations hurled his way by liberals, terming him a bully, un-serious candidate, and a politician hell bent on playing divisive politics for personal gain.

However, the same candor that has ruffled many a liberal figure in the United States of America's media and political circles has also won him several loyalists among Republicans.

His frankness, ability to call a spade a spade without resorting to a trademark diplomacy and capacity to self-fund his political campaigns has ensured a steady following and plenty of exposure. The wide spread news coverage, and endorsements in popular media outlets has drawn sufficient public attention to his campaign.

Powerful Rhetoric

Trump has always been perceptive and shrewd enough to run his campaign based on exceptionally strong rhetoric that has brought him scores of admirers. From reversing seemingly unfavorable taxes to a more prevalent use of Merry Christmas over Happy Holidays, Trump has showed glowing support for Christians in the U.S.

Other noteworthy issues highlighted in his campaign, which his spoke very sternly and vocally about, comprise caring for military veterans, making the U.S. armed forces stronger, intimidation of Mideast terrorist group ISIS through aggressive bombings and attacks, monitoring specific mosques in the country, forging trade agreements more beneficial for American workers.

You may or may not agree with his views, but you've got to hand it over to the man for not veiling his true views in the garb of diplomacy and political correctness. As businessman and politician, the biggest lessons to imbibe from his life are a characteristic fearlessness and forthrightness. It's no secret that Trump's outspoken spirit and brazenness has made him a presidential candidate well worth considering among the other political stalwarts.

Immigration Policies

One of Donald Trump's most critical election agendas includes the highly debated immigration policies. He has spoken about making U.S. border security stronger, which included a controversial vow to build a wall between Mexico and the United States of America to avoid infiltration of illegal immigrants onto American soil.

Though largely favorable to the U.S. working class, the policies were ripped apart by experts for their practicality and efficiency. He also vowed to create a deportation force to send back around 11 million people unlawfully residing in the U.S. He is also a staunch opponent of birthright citizenship, arguing that simply taking birth in the United States shouldn't naturally qualify a person for U.S. citizenship.

War on Terrorism

One of his most controversial and highly publicized proposals included a momentary ban on Muslims immigrating to the United States. This was a direct reaction to the series of attacks in Europe by radical Islamic groups. The proposal earned him plenty of flak, since his opponents argued it went against basic American values and the right awarded to individuals by the Constitution.

In the wake of negative publicity, Trump softened his stand a bit by going on record to state the ban would only be applicable for people with a proven track record of terrorism against the U.S. or its diplomatic allies. The ban, according to Trump, would be lifted when the U.S. government had mastered the system of screening out prospective terrorists.

The Pope Controversy

In February 2016 while returning from Mexico, the Pope, referring to Donald Trump, reportedly told the media that anyone talking about building walls instead of bridges cannot be a true Christian, if he (Trump) meant things in a particular way.

Trump hit back at the Pope stating that the Mexican government was using him (the Pope) as a mere pawn for political gain for continuously ripping off the United States. Trump also went on to say that if the ISIL (Islamic State) ever launches an attack on the Vatican, the Pope will wish Trump was the president, since the attack would never have happened under his presidency.

The Pope's office swiftly swung into action to issue a statement emphasizing that the Pope was not launching any attack on Trump or attempting to sway voters. It also mentioned that media headlines in the U.S. were exaggerated beyond what the Pope actually said. Matters came to a settle when Trump acknowledged the fact that the media reported beyond what the Pope originally said and meant.

Chapter 7:
Facts We Bet You Didn't Know
About Donald Trump

- Donald Trump, as opposed his absolutely flamboyant personality and aggressive demeanor, is a teetotaler and claims to have never done any drugs or smoked a cigarette in his life. How's that for some healthy discipline?

- A self-confessed germophobe, he despises shaking hands with people. When it gets awkward and he's compelled to greet the other person, trump merely pulls the person close to the body.

- Though he's made some astute business decisions over the years, Donald Trump has also missed some spectacular investment opportunities. He had the option of buying the Patriots, a popular Football team in 1988. Well, he believed then that it wasn't a very sound investment. The team is worth over $2 billion today. Just goes to show, he's human too, and like the rest of us sometimes fails to recognize the true potential of an opportunity.

- Donald Trump was financial advisor to Mike Tyson and even went on to host Tyson's bout against Michael Spinks at the sprawling Atlantic City.

- He is an avid golfer and an active member of the Winged Foot Golf Club in Mamaroneck, New York. Trump often plays at the golf courses his company owns and runs.

- He is the sole presidential candidate to have an entire board game dedicated to him, called Trump: The Game. Such is the appeal of his brand in popular culture.

- Few know that Trump actually won a worst supporting actor Razzie for the 1989 turkey "Ghosts Can't Do I."

- Believe it or faint, Donald Trump actually uses a haircare product manufactured by Farouk Systems known as Hetmel Hair. He swears by the goodness of the $16 hairspray.

- In true Godfather style, he made an offer that was almost too difficult to refuse when he offered Barack Obama a lifetime membership at his golf courses if the latter resigned from his presidency. Talk about being a tough negotiator.

- Now this is straight out of a soap opera. After Donald cheated on his wife Iavana Trump with actress Marla Maples, the two partners dramatically came face to face in Aspen where Maples is said to have famously asked Ivana if she (Ivana) was in love with her husband. "Because I am", Maples stated emphatically.

- While we lesser mortals take great pleasure by eating pizza with our bare hands, Donald Trump likes eating his pizza only with a fork and knife. It's more comfortable and less messy according to him. He also doesn't fancy eating the crust. I feel like a barbarian already.

- His real family name is Drumpf and not Trump as it has currently evolved into. Surprising, isn't it? Considering how he's an ardent proponent of the idea of staunchly sticking to your family name. Guess, the name just gradually evolved and he couldn't help it because he had no role in changing it.

Chapter 8:
Donald Trump's Net Worth

Forbes has pegged Donald Trump's net worth at 4.5 billion, while *Bloomberg* has estimated it be around 2.9 billion. The man himself claims to be worth more than ten billion dollars. These differences can be attributed to fluctuations in estimates of property value. The evaluation makes Trump one of the wealthiest politicians in the history of America, and #336 on *Forbes* list of the world's richest people in March 2016.

Trump first made his way into the *Forbes* list of the world's wealthiest movers and shakers in 1982, when he was said to be worth $200 million, which included a share from his father's net worth. He featured consistently on the list for several years until his financial disorderliness cost him his position on the list from 1990 till about 1995. In April 2011, it was largely speculated that Trump would run for presidency in the 2012 election. However, this was later debunked when Donald Trump stayed away from contesting for presidential elections in 2012. However, what followed was an elaborate financial disclosure that was converted into a published paperback that pinned Donald Trump's net worth at $7 billion.

In June, 2015, just before Trump announced his candidature for presidency, he went on to release a full page financial disclosure put together by one of biggest accounting firms that stated his net worth was around $8,737,540,000. *Forbes* simply dismissed that Trump's claims are nothing but an exaggerated estimate of his wealth.

In July, 2015, election regulators made public details about Trump's reported wealth and holdings when he sought a Republican presidential candidature, which revealed his assets to be over $1.4 billion, including $70 million worth of stocks, and $265 million in debt. Getting a totally accurate estimate of Donald Trump's net worth is a near impossible and impractical task with fluctuations in real estate evaluations, his on-going royalties and other difficult to track income sources, and existing assets.

Forbes went on to reduce Trump's estimated net worth by $125 million immediately after his controversial take on illegal Mexican immigrants that spelled the termination of his contracts with NBC Universal, Macy's, Perfumania, PVH, Univision and Serta.

His dropped ratings in 2015 hint at the market challenges that could lie ahead for his myriad ventures. But knowing the man's persona, it doesn't look like he's going to be bogged down for long and will bounce back even more spiritedly following the temporary business setbacks. He looks like he's alright with his business taking a back seat for the larger presidency goal.

Chapter 9: Entrepreneurial Lessons From Donald Trump's Stable

While we did get a sneak peak at the infallible man's journey, here are some important lessons that we can imbibe from Trump's business life. He's known to do and say some of the most deep-seated things and that kind of sums up the mindset almost every businessman should channelize productively. To never settle for being anything, but the best.

There are no Consolation Prizes in the Real World

If observed closely, Trump's life has never been about mere participation. He participates to win. Period. Though we've been deeply ingrained in the philosophy of participation being good enough, Trump has taken the idea by its horns to prove nothing is greater than victory and that there are no consolation prizes in real life. You play to win.

Donald Trump has jumped into the presidential foray to win the election. He doesn't seek to build resorts that are referred to as one of the best. He strives to make it THE BEST. Excelling and playing to win are some of the most marked characteristics of Trump as a businessman.

Universal Appeal is a Myth

Whether in business or his presidential campaign, Donald Trump has never sought to appeal to everyone. He has had his share of critics, competitors and detractors both in the business and political world, but he's stayed true to his beliefs/products.

Trump understood early on that it's not humanly possible to please everyone and that one should rather be true to themselves than falsely appeal to all and sundry. He has mastered the art of indentifying his market/target audience and then has gone about specifically focusing on them to achieve his goals. It's a losing fight if you seek to pander everyone, over appealing to a select few.

Confidence, Confidence and More Confidence

Donald Trump is the epitome of confidence and it shows in everything from his bold speeches, to his daring ventures, to strategic business ideas. He has tremendous confidence in his abilities and beliefs, from which stems his capacity to make solid decisions. A huge portion of his success as an entrepreneur can be attributed to his innate sense of self-confidence. Trump oozes confidence when he talks, and makes decisions. Believing in your abilities to manifest powerful goals is the first path on the highway to success.

When you begin each day with the mindset of winning, your actions are in sync with those winsome thoughts, and more often than not, you end up winning. You have channelized your mental faculties and energy towards victory and this overflowing confidence sets you apart from unsure competitors. Entrepreneurship is as much a mindset game as it is about toiling hard and possessing superior organization skills.

Try telling Donald Trump that his plan isn't workable, and hear him give a full throated laugh. He always believes he will win, and more often than not, he does. This confidence alone separates billionaires from the strugglers.

Forge a Powerful Brand Early in the Game

The brand 'Donald Trump' is a force to reckon with. There's no disputing that. From establishing himself as a strong proponent of the making America powerful again to building solid real estate and entertainment brands, Trump has never failed to recognize the value of a brand early on and cash in on it.

He has always driven home the point that you have to entrench the flag of your brand deeply in the ethos of your customer's lives. The brand should signify their lifestyle, and something they take great pride in. From the iconic Trump Tower to the swish holiday resorts to beauty pageants, to the presidential run, Donald Trump's life can be summed up in two words – The Brand.

He recognized the need and potential of several businesses early on and transformed them into major brands, thus giving him the pioneering edge of launching path-breaking business models that set the precedent for many duplicates.

Donald Trump aggressively leveraged the power of the Trump brand by marketing several products and business ventures under it. Trump Financial, Trump Restaurants, Donald. J. Trump signature range, Trump Sales and Leasing, and more. He owns a mock-up business game known as Donald Trump's Real Estate Tycoon and pocketed a cool $1.5 million for each hour long presentation on The Learning Apex platform.

Conflict Leads to Growth

Most successful people do not shy away from conflict and in fact embrace it as a means of growth and transformation. Donald Trump embraces conflict, and often views it as an opportunity rather than a threat. He believes conflicts provide a large perspective and multi-dimensional view of an existing issue.

Conflicts are part of the eco system of business organizations, and are sometimes necessary to maintain a healthy balance. They help you evolve, make better decisions, broaden your horizon and grow your enterprise. Entrepreneurs boxed in by their beliefs of suppressing/fearing conflict seldom soar high. Lack of conflict means lack of opportunities to think of alternatives, which simply translates into stagnation.

Bounce Backs

Donald Trump was heavily drowned in debt in the 1990's. Did he believe he was done with for good? No sir. While most businessmen would be intimidated and demoralized by the heavy setbacks in business, our man quickly gathers himself brushes off the dust and goes about building bigger businesses. While playing safe and sinking into your comfort zone seems like a cushy proposition, only those who have the courage to bounce back witness stellar results.

When the going gets tough in life and business, we often forget to count our blessings. We forget to focus on the pros and brood over the cons. Donald Trump doesn't quite comprehend the idea of giving up. Like a champion, he continues to play even though the field conditions are not always ideal. He keeps coming back for more after momentary setbacks, because as he himself has been quoted as saying, "Sometimes by losing a battle you find a new way to win the war."

Thinking Big

Donald Trump's philosophy has always been, if you are thinking something, you might as well think big. His plans have never been anything short of ambitious and grand. Whether it was negotiating strategic ways to fund his mammoth real estate projects to his foray into the entertainment industry, everything has been larger than life. He's never shied away from thinking and implementing big.

What could be a better testimony of thinking big other than the awe-inspiring Trump Tower in New York City? Trump thinks big and chases his vision with the tenacity of a possessed individual. If you keep aside your political beliefs, you can objectively see why the man's such a natural leader and a big entrepreneurial success.

Turn Your Passion into Money

If there's a single most valuable lesson to be taken from Donald Trump's life and business, it is putting your energy into something that you are extremely driven or enthusiastic about. Trump had once famously stated that he doesn't merely negotiate business deals for monetary gain but because he does it simply for the passion of doing it.

Whatever you are doing, if there's no passion for doing it, the determination to pull through in challenging times won't last for long. The energy, passion and enthusiasm you possess for any idea/venture will go a long way in helping you make a success of it.

Positive energy and positive thoughts often translate into positive and fulfilling results. If art makes your world go around, try to discover how you can monetize it. Similarly, if it's a sport of hobby that you are exceptionally good at or passionate about, harness ways to generate income from it. There's a lot of money lying on the table, if only we realize our true potential and how to get it into our pockets.

If You've Created it – Roll It

Once Donald Trump recognized the value of his real estate, there was no stopping him. Business began to explode. Not only did he successfully apply the licensing model (which contributes a huge amount to his company's aggregated profits) to his real estate empire, but also applied it to other sectors to diversify his source of income.

Trump has vigorously and enthusiastically tapped into the highly lucrative passive income licensing model to generate consistent profits for his company. He knows how to roll his brand name itself for money. Forget about products or services, his brand name alone rakes in millions. This is one of the most lucrative business models to take note of from Donald Trump's life.

Make Everyone Feel Like a Star

Trump makes himself a star unfailingly, but he also makes everyone else around him feel like a star. Ever noticed how he conducted himself on *The Apprentice*. Every time the team won a challenge, they bagged an enviable reward such as dinner at exclusive eateries. Trump realizes the importance of making everyone feel special for the success of a venture. He understands that by making others feel special; he is increasing his own appeal and brand value.

Chapter 10:
Marketing Lessons to Be Learnt from Trump's Presidential Campaign

Like him or not, agree with him or not, there are plenty of invaluable lessons you can learn from Donald Trump's presidential campaign. Other than being a strong force in the race, the man has commanded worldwide media spotlight for his campaign.

Despite his seemingly arrogant disposition and high-handed ways, the business mogul continues to make headlines day after day. The polls keep rising in his favor, and there's a powerful buzz about him everywhere. Here are some precious marketing lessons we can take note of from his campaigns.

Understand Your Audience Well

Donald Trump has selectively identified his audience and is playing to them. He doesn't care one bit about whether everyone loves, or agrees with, or favors him. Trump knows he's not part of a popularity contest, and is catering only to a selected group of voters who believe in his ideology.

His dismissal of expert opinions and popularity polls is nothing but his core belief that your brand doesn't have to appeal to everyone, but should address the concerns of your audience in an impactful and relevant manner.

He has positioned himself as the voice of several disillusioned Republicans who are hopeful about reclaiming the White House. Trump is unabashedly and candidly sharing their feelings. Identify your target audience, talk of their concerns, and present solutions to address these concerns. Isn't that what astute marketing is all about?

Don't Apologize for Everything

Trump is unlike any presidential candidate you've ever witnessed. He absolutely stands by his words, and does so without any feelings of remorse or shame. He says it like he feels it, and has no qualms in articulating views that would otherwise be considered politically incorrect. Donald Trump doesn't take his critics too seriously, and has never apologized for his controversial stances.

As a marketer, it's hard to know where to stop when it comes to admitting your mistakes and apologizing to customers. You have to maintain a fine balance between protecting your brand's reputation and spending all your energy and efforts on trying to please every unhappy customer. Apologizing every time when an apology is unwarranted can irrevocably sully your brand image. In addition to happy customers, you also have the responsibility of upholding your brand's posture.

Trump epitomizes a bold, no-holds barred kind of marketing approach that is clear headed and refuses to bow down to popular dictates. There's no 'sorry' for Trump. He just moves from one deal to another, and some may find that a refreshing lesson from the hackneyed please all your customers approach.

Audacity Can Be Good Sometimes

Trump has said several audacious things during his campaign, from controversial statements about illegal Mexican immigrants to inflammatory speeches about radical Islamic outfits. However, every new faux pas in a speech earns him widespread coverage and remarkably boosts his poll performance. Even if he's not being gentle or courteous, his supporters hand it over to him for being truthful. He's in your face and telling you things like he sees it and feels it.

That's not to reinforce that any publicity is good publicity for your brand. It merely points to the fact that even when things are not very popular, often bordering on controversial, as a marketer it is important to keep it real.

Far too many businesses aim to go mainstream by appealing to everyone. It's perfectly alright to let go of some customers who just don't get the value of your products/services if you are playing to a certain niche audience who swear by your products/services.

Trust Your Brand

Trump doesn't flinch when it comes to trusting his brand completely. What makes him appealing for fellow Republicans is that he not only articulates their stand brazenly, but does so in a rather unrefined and unrehearsed manner.

His speeches don't come across as carefully planned and practiced, but rather spur of the moment words about whatever he's feeling strongly about at the time. He is fully aware of his brand value, the power he yields on his audience, and doesn't believe in testing messages for their efficacy with clinical mechanisms that kill the spontaneity of the message.

It is vital to trust your brand and sometimes make intuitive decisions based on a firm belief in your brand, rather than undertaking elaborate focus group studies that disconnect your product/service from its real audience. Testing is good, but too much reliance on testing over intuitively knowing the pulse of your audience can spoil the game for you.

Connect With Your Audience Emotionally

It's no secret that Donald Trump has gathered a passionately loyal following. You may agree with him or not, but you can't deny the fact that he has earned himself a feverish bunch of supporters because he's tugged at their emotional strings brilliantly.

He's got them angry, provoked, frustrated and disgruntled to drive home his point. With every speech, tweet and elaborate rant he piques some raw emotions in his followers that are quickly lapped up by them. Marketing is nothing but a dexterous balance of logic and emotion to appeal to your audience.

The emotional quotient has for long been a marketer's favorite tool to capture the imagination and attention of his audience, and position his product/service as a solution to the audience's most compelling problems. Donald Trump's presidential campaign only reinforces this surefire marketing strategy.

Blow Your Own Trumpet

Trump never misses an opportunity to talk about how he's leading the polls, or how rich he is or just how smart he is. He will make you believe that there's no one smarter, richer and more popular than him in the universe with his smooth ability to blow his own trumpet (no pun intended).

Businessmen are often intimidated by the prospect of confidently endorsing their successes. They don't think much about extolling the virtues of their own brand and prefer letting customers do the talking.

However, success stories and highlighting the remarkable selling points of your products/services are crucial for building strong brands. You have to capture the attention of prospective customers and convert them into loyal buyers by raving about your products/services.

Every entrepreneur has to believe his product is nothing short of fantastic to make his audiences believe the same. Emphasize your success stories, positive customer reviews, and benefits of your product/service to inspire attention for your products/services over several others in the market.

De-position the Opposition

Trump absolutely upstaged his opponent Hillary Clinton and hogged the media celebrity limelight with his frank and forthright opinions. Are you doing enough to make your competitors look irrelevant and average? Are you simply focused on following prevailing trends on re-inventing the wheel? Do you see yourself as just one of the businesses that functions within your field or are you creating a path-breaking model for others to emulate?

As much as it is about extolling his own virtues, Trump's campaign is also about throwing his opponents campaign off the gear to position himself as the only solution to America's existing woes. You have to identify the demerits of your competitors and build on your own products/services to fill in the gap for those demerits. You have to be perceptive enough to spot their weaknesses and build your marketing campaigns around it.

Harness the Power of Social Media

Anyone who follows Donald Trump on Twitter will know how his feed is exploding with controversial Tweets and inflammatory opinions. This ensures sufficient free media coverage and draws people in droves at his rallies.

While you may argue about the general sentiment in the media being negative about Trump's social media posts, it increases his organic reach nevertheless. Donald Trump has acquired a reach that is way greater than that of his competitors by harnessing the power of the social media for creating and strengthening popular public opinion. Trump has recognized the virtue of new age media and is effectively disseminating his message to his target audience.

If there's one lesson savvy marketers can take back from Donald Trump's social media accounts, it's that when used in combination with other channels, social media can be a compelling and entertaining platform for grabbing the attention of your target audience.

Rather than treating it as just another marketing platform, build on the fact that you can have a direct conversation with thousands of customers all over the world in about 140 well-written characters.

Try and speak in the voice of your potential customers. Stay entertaining, current, relevant, funny and emotional. Create posts that inspire conversation and customer engagement. Involve your audience in your message. Donald Trump seldom fails to do that.

Summing It Up

In the end, Donald Trump is all about taking your chances, knowing how to harness the power of your brand, reaching out to your audience by tugging at their emotions, being audacious, staying spontaneous and unrehearsed, being unapologetic, dethroning the opposition, revealing exceptionally high confidence, understanding your audience and using the power of social media to have a direct connection with your audience.

Chapter 11:
Donald Trump's Books

Some of the most famous books authored and co-authored by Donald Trump include *Trump: The Art of the Deal, Trump: The Art of Survival, The America We Deserve, Trump: How to Get Rich, Think Big and Kick Ass in Business and Life, Trump 101: The Way to Success, Midas Touch: Why Some Entrepreneurs Get Rich – and Why Most Don't* and many more.

In the *Art of the Deal,* Trump's most popular book, he talks about the time tested strategies and techniques he's used to negotiate a string of high-profile deals. It reads more like an autobiography of Trump's life, spanning from his Brooklyn beginnings to his first successful Swifton Village deal, to his early-career trophies such as the Trump Tower in New York City.

In 2004, he came up with another book to cash in on the success of *The Apprentice. How to Get Rich* succeeded in reinforcing his brand of being a wealth creation and business guru. It catered to aspiring billionaires hooked to reality TV. The book is peppered with plenty of anecdotes and stories to highlight his business savvy image

In *Trump: The Art of a Comeback* the entrepreneur talks about his various business failures, and how he resurrected his empire despite the setbacks. Even while talking of his business challenges, Trump maintains a positive attitude, a hopeful approach and the ability to focus on opportunities over challenges. While the first chapter is devoted to the business problems faced by Trump's business ventures, the others are exhaustive narratives about his personal life as well the several complicated deals he has pulled though.

In *Think Like a Billionaire,* Trump not only tantalizes you with the prospect of turning you into a billionaire but also offers you some amazing diet tips. Some random pieces of advice from the book include always remembering people's names, being on time, and thoroughly inspecting a home before purchasing it. There's also a predictably short section on "How to be Married" (he wouldn't be an ace at this for sure).

In *The America We Deserve,* though authored in 2000, Trump comes as close to his presidential campaign avatar of 2016 as ever. It reveals that his underlying xenophobia and fear of foreigners influencing the country's economy is not some craftily created campaign strategy, but the core political ideology on which his entire campaign rests.

Donald Trump expresses grave concerns over the phenomenon of globalization and reiterates the fact that even if it makes him an America-firster, he will always strive hard to protect the employment of American families. Much of his current campaign agenda based on tackling illegal immigrants in the U.S. and banning the outsourcing of American jobs to overseas markets stems from the beliefs expresses in *The America We Deserve.*

The book chronicles his apprehensions about America's excessive engagement in world politics. It also lists his views on a mishmash of topics and federal policies that he doesn't care much about. Its gives a good background of the man as we know him today.

Conclusion

Thanks again for taking the time to read this book!

You should now have a good understanding of Donald Trump and his life journey!

If you enjoyed this book, please take the time to leave me a review on Amazon. I appreciate your honest feedback, and it really helps me to continue producing high quality books.